ON THE ROAD

Text copyright © Claire Llewellyn 2006
Illustrations copyright © Mike Gordon 2006

First published by Hodder Children's Books in 2006
Reprinted in 2006

This paperback edition published in 2007 by Wayland,
an imprint of Hachette Children's Books

Editor: Kirsty Hamilton
Designer: Peter Bailey, Proof Books
Digital Colour Designer: Carl Gordon

British Library Cataloguing in Publication Data
Llewellyn, Claire
Look out on the road
1.Pedestrian accidents – Prevention – Pictorial works –
Juvenile literature 2.Cycling accidents – Prevention –
Pictorial works – Juvenile literature
I.Title II.Gordon, Mike III.On the road
613.6

Printed in China

ISBN-13: 978 0 7502 5289 8

Hachette Children's Books
338 Euston Road,
London NW1 3BH

LOOK OUT!
ON THE ROAD

Written by Claire Llewellyn

Illustrated by Mike Gordon

WAYLAND

We all use roads from time to time.

When we're out on our bike ...

catching a bus ...

or driving in
the car.

There are all kinds of vehicles on the roads – lorries, taxis, police cars, vans.

All this traffic makes the roads very busy.

7

Cars, trucks and vans are powerful machines. They are fast and very heavy.

Look what happens when they hit something.

What could happen if they hit you?

Roads are very dangerous places.
When you're walking along them,
it's important to be careful.

Stay on the pavement, next to an adult.
What could happen if you ran ahead?

Sometimes we have to cross the road. This can be tricky and needs a lot of care.

Luckily, there are places that make it safer.

Always choose the safest place to cross the road. A good place is a pelican crossing.

Can I push the button?

You push the button to change the lights. How do you know when it is safe to go?

A zebra crossing is another good place to cross. Zebra crossings don't have buttons or lights.

You wait on the pavement until the traffic stops.

This may take a moment or two. Cars need time to slow down and stop.

How do you know when it is safe to go?

Sometimes you need to cross
the road and there are no
special crossings.

This is a nuisance if you
want to cross quickly to
see a friend or to buy
an ice-cream.

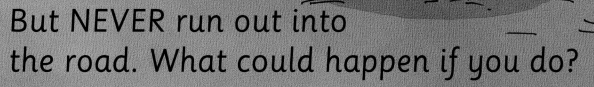

But NEVER run out into
the road. What could happen if you do?

19

Always cross the road safely. First, find a place where you can see the road clearly.

I can't see. Let's go down a bit.

Then, stop by the kerb and look both ways. Listen for traffic, too.

When the road is empty, walk straight across, and look and listen as you go.

When you walk along roads at night, you need to take special care.

Drivers cannot see you well in the dark.

How can you make yourself stand out? How can you make yourself safe?

Can you keep yourself safe when you're in a car? Everyone has to wear a seatbelt –

the driver ...

the passengers ...

and baby, too.

A seatbelt helps to keep you safe.

What could happen if you
didn't wear one?

Have you ever played on the pavement?

Playing outside is a lot of fun, but what could happen if you slipped off the kerb, or chased a ball into the road?

Roads are not the best places to play.
Can you think of anywhere safer?

Roads are busy, dangerous places.
But we can all learn to use
them safely.

Keep looking ...

keep listening ...

keep safe!

Notes for parents and teachers

Look Out! On the Road and the National Curriculum

This book will help cover elements of the PSHE curriculum at KS1 (ages 5-7), in particular the requirement that children at this age "should be taught … rules for, and ways of, keeping safe, including basic road safety, and about people who can help them to stay safe". The Citizenship KS1 and KS2 schemes of work are also relevant. Activities relating to the scheme of work unit entitled 'People who help us – the local police' could include personal safety elements and road safety.

Issues raised in the book

Look Out! On the Road is intended to be an enjoyable book that discusses the importance of road safety. Throughout, children are given the opportunity to think independently about what might happen if they do not pay attention to road safety issues. It allows them time to explore these issues and discuss them with their family, class and school. It encourages them to think about safety first and how they can make themselves safe.

The book looks at vehicles that go on the road – cars, trucks, vans etc. It asks questions about what happens when cars hit something, especially what happens if a person is hit by a vehicle.

It is also full of situations that children and adults will have encountered. It allows a child to ask and answer questions on a one-to-one basis with you. How can you make yourself clearly visible to drivers? How can you make yourself safe? The illustrations help with ideas and suggestions.

Being safe on the road is important for everyone. Can your children think of an incident in which they have crossed a road between two cars, or been unable to find a safe place to cross? How did this make them feel? The book tackles these and many other issues. It uses open-ended questions to encourage children to think for themselves about the consequences of their behaviour.

Suggested follow-up activities

Try doing a traffic survey to see how many cars, trucks etc. go along the road. Make a picture collection of different types of vehicles and display them in a book or on a wall.

Investigate which materials make good reflectors by using a torch in a dark box.

Act out scenes of people trying to cross busy roads, either on a car mat or in the playground. Children could take different roles as cars, vans, pedestrians etc.

Invite a 'lollipop' person into school and interview him or her about road safety issues. Alternatively, contact your local road safety officer to come to school and talk to the children.

The Royal Society for the Prevention of Accidents (ROSPA) has a useful and informative website including fact sheets: www.rospa.com

Books to read

Safety First: On the Road (Franklin Watts, 2004)
Look Out on the Road (Evans Brothers, 2003)